JAZZ ER CISE IS A LAN G UAGE

gabriel
ojeda-sague

the operating system c. 2018

the operating system print//document

Jazzercise is a Language

ISBN: 978-1-946031-19-8
Library of Congress Control Number: 2018930480

This text was set in Avenir Next Ultra Light, Air Conditioner, Minion, Franchise, and OCR-A Standard, printed and bound by Spencer Printing, in Honesdale, PA, in the USA. Books from The Operating System are distributed to the trade by SPD/Small Press Distribution, with ePub and POD via Ingram.

This book was edited and designed by Lynne DeSilva-Johnson, with assistant copyediting by Kenyatta JP García.

Front and back covers use original photographs by Liz Barr c. 2017
Learn more about her work and purchase prints at http://liz-barr.com

the operating system
141 Spencer Street #203
Brooklyn, NY 11205
www.theoperatingsystem.org
operator@theoperatingsystem.org

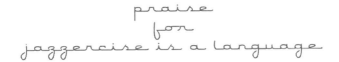
praise
for
jazzercise is a language

"Jazzercise — the dance-inspired exercise regime popular in the 1980s — may seem a thin hook for an entire book of ambitious verse and prose poems about bodies and sex and 'gender-discordant' identity, melancholy and capitalism and mortality. But Ojeda-Sague definitely, and defiantly, makes it work. In raggedly bisected verse, in squares of prose, and in cascading columns of type, this magnificently bizarre project presents the internal monologue of a queer Latinx exercise-tape viewer, making promises to himself, critiquing other (largely white) viewers, mixing humor with provocation and both with non sequiturs: 'You're loving this, right: swing those arms: are / you smiling: when you're smiling I know you're / breathing: I can tell you that a century of protests / is to come.' Ojeda-Sague acts out and attempts the impossible: 'I hate a lake I eat a stop / sign as told I could be a receipt.' His short phrases pivot dizzyingly between things you might say while working out to music, and things no one would quite say: 'we were born in a fishbowl: / we grew up eating Cheerios: we loved our / husbands.' Yet Ojeda-Sague does not mock the Jazzercisers. Instead, as if mimicking workout instructors, Ojeda-Sague gives himself directions, showing what it would take to change a society built on patriarchy and white privilege, and what it would take to change his mind. 'Let all your friends / know the same secret,' he advises, 'then change / that aspect of yourself / without telling them. … this will strengthen / your squat / and open your breath.'"

STEPHANIE BURT, NEW YORK TIMES BOOK REVIEW
"IN RECENT POETRY COLLECTIONS, WEAPONS MADE OF WORDS"

Through the syntax and vocabulary of a dance style proselytized by one, sweaty-sexy, hyper-affirmative Jazzercise camp leader Judi Sheppard Missett, *Jazzercise Is a Language* reveals multiple and violent registers of racial and cultural interpellation: "I determine the circumstance of my own abduction." Behind the seemingly benign landscape of "six white women stepping to the left," I encountered, strangely and briefly, the little Japanese girl in me with the overwhelming aspiration to be a perfectly shaped, beautiful white lady shimmying in a leotard. Gabriel Ojeda-Sague leads us into the complicated discussion of how we got here by pivoting back to the ever contracting-and-releasing dance around the semantic body, all the way back to the secret that "is in the derrière, the burning secret, the bushel of flowers," where we burn - and burn - and burn - Do you feel it? I do.

SAWAKO NAKUYASU

The slinky style of Jazzercise founder Judi Sheppard Missett haunts this book of poems by Philadelphia-based wunderkind Gabriel Ojeda-Sague. I had not thought I remembered Judi, but a few pages into the volume she returns to grip me again, her patented blend of syncopation, disco beat, showbiz honey with a drop of vinegar, sex appeal tease. She sings like the laziest gal in town, Dietrich crossed with Keely Smith, but her body was simultaneously commanding the whole world to work it. Her position as a boss of a posse of backup employees also interests the poet, whose POV shifts mimic and question the status of Sheppard Missett's musicality and even of exercise itself. The demands of the social world on the body are Ojeda-Sague's persistent theme: the shame and fear on which every exercise empire is built, the potential for subverting these tropes by paying attention to the once abjured vehicle of VCR Jazzercise tapes—its grain and pastel and stray pixels—the power and strength and endurance of being gay and of color in the middle of such a disco. I had trouble imagining this book when he was describing it to me, but now that it's in my hands, it reads as one of the absolute essentials of our moment in poetry.

KEVIN KILLIAN

Jazzercise Is a Language is rich with original music and a mysteriously evocative internal movement. It brings us closer to a future magic formed by the tropical energies some of us might keep in our interiors, even if that magic were initially only relatable through the presence of a rooster. Gabriel Ojeda-Sague's poems are 'song[s that] lie sweetly on the wound.' He shape-shifts his interior and exterior selves like the oceans do, and shows us not only that the universe is always speaking to us, but also that it is always speaking to itself in us. I am relieved and renewed as if from a good night of powerful and gentle dreams when I read his poems.

ROBERTO HARRISON

JAZZERCISE

IS

A

LANGUAGE

to my mother

"Cause everything I have in the world has many, many insecurities."

LYPSINKA,
"The Passion of the Crawford"

Again: the sound of a body being thrown to the ground: four on the floor

Landscape of white women swinging for shoulder tension: dynamic stretch: last one: all in the hips with voices exhausted from breathing: leave your arms right here, gentle and unopposed: leave your arms right here, where I can see them: for heaven's sake: 1969: life with an anaerobe: a high-impact sixty minutes: enough not to be clothing, but eventually a curved program

Do you know what it's like to have the arm shrink
away: how it is to lose the stomach: to have your
right eye hidden away under a stone: come up
again: rip apart the line: chassé: the megaphone
blasts into seven white ears: important like small
poinsettias

Push sound away like washing your hair: imagine
these hips biting the feeling: dream like you are
dreaming the body burn: twist to twist the body
away: do you notice my sneakers: an assembly
of mad lines

Will motors overrun the populace: are you ready for V's: I kick out my boyfriend because I want to lose the faith: pink Chelsea astride the silver dollar lays her hair into tar: she's blonde but only on video: blonde even to the roots: blonde in the way only blonde is blonde: blonde in a way that can save the world: so blonde it arms the populace: set your backpack into the lonely hole

Again: fit Susan: Rebecca always dancing: the bragging Lisa of all my distant dreams: mirage of teacups: bumping shoulders across a long, wild span of grass: the string of endless lights in a windmill: I want a body that points its toes across a coast

Just relax, it's a nice, easy breeze: lengthen your spine: open: really feel the reach: that's my favorite stretch: I really mean it: I know we're in a stuffy studio, but don't you feel like you can feel the sun

What I really want is that ponytail, is a pink sports bra, is black leggings, is make-up that never sweats through, is power over men and to have their power over me, is the feeling of always holding a stretch: I want to be a woman who releases the stretch after a long count

Again:

Have you noticed you synthesize like an agent,
like a small possum: one day, I opened my closet
and noticed all I had was pink tank-tops inside
and I blamed my lover for it: so, turn your hip,
don't feel embarrassed: you're trying to body
burn: you can do that, I promise

In all the old Jazzercise tapes it's the same way: all white women except for one brown-skinned woman: she's always to the back and to the right: the finest moments are when she suddenly stops smiling, the one they notably named Maria, who stands out against a white background: at one point, the white lead says again "let's do that samba" and there's an instant, however small, where Maria goes off-beat: I feel most white when I smile at white people

Again:

General admission of my fault, cosmically: I don't miss a spot: I have been taught not to look directly into set lights, or even indirectly at their plastic frames: keep control in your shoulders, like it was in the 80s: the burning still smells like my mom's old living room: crowds of headbands loosen their grip: insistent perfume

Smile and do it: if stories simulated the way video does, I'd guide the festive family into falling action: a powder blue mirage in my time of need: discs fuming through the muscles you use so diligently: squeeze, tighten, square: if only all our bodies were perfect squares, pixels in the burn

Where you meet the melody, an intimate touch never lopsided: it's jazz, so we should never touch the floor: salvo of purple legs, or a keyboard: the secret is in the derriere, the burning secret, the bushel of flowers

You're loving this, right: swing those arms: are you smiling: when you're smiling I know you're breathing: I can tell you that a century of protests is to come: we are about to live fifty years of saxophone rage: I saw all of it in the stars: in cards: I saw it there behind the shortest handle, the shortest curtain, caution in the hamstring: a production of exercise, an exercise of video, a video and burning correspondence: the grains will pass, even if it takes twisting the knob

Remember who you are doing all this for: the man behind the counter who believes in sainthood: those cute little hands that stretch out to the sky: but here, in my life, the sky is fluorescent bulbs, it's plaster ceiling, it's where the next room starts

Richard Simmons is an American myth, but jazz is not: Jazzercise is a complex of borrowed cultural sites pulled together into the infrastructure of physical literacy: Judi Sheppard Missett falls into a vat of seltzer: under her hairline bubbles my secret formula

Go ahead Susie, let me see the drums: medium cardiovascular to waistline: striped leotard I offer to orixas, covered in a thick layer of honey: I am a massive circle, but as she says "the bigger the circle, the smaller the waist"

What body changes under green light: or yellow
light: or red: or the seeping of leotards into a
big, dark space where the ball-change snaps:
single, single, double: what personhood eats
out the little light clambering and clambering

The man says it's "just" that, as if something is
something and not another too: I cool you down,
I cool you down: surely in that studio they can't
feel winter wind gnawing the side of my face:
a singed ring around my nostrils: just overage:
I took myself into my brother's room and gave
myself a shiny new name

I twist out the little fears caught in my hair: I'm suddenly as sweaty as I've ever wanted to be, which is how I know I've reached "intimate": to pump it up: I promise it's not ball-and-chains, it's just leg-warmers: 2 and 2 and 2 and 2 and 2 and 2 and 2 and 2

I've gotten to know the tunnel blonde hair takes out of a white woman's head: I kept all the filthy socks in a black box under my bed: burrow lips in elbows, the secrets: Jazzercise is built on import, by force: pressured down by midi: build a white woman's body with "samba," "mambo," "salsa," "jazz," "bop": whose buttons get pushed: you know, some videos don't even try to include a single person of color: do we not exercise: wear leotards: wear headbands: do we not shimmy and chassé: body talk and body burn

Next, we'll do a move called the "Soul Sister": will you love me on a sunny day: if my body gets smaller: if I can look like the young John Travolta: if I do the next cha-cha step: will you love me if I pull the straps to the right part of my waist so my body looks like it's made of disparate connectable parts

The skin separates a bit at the toes: the blood bubbles while the hips roll: visible bones: the hair from two girls gets tangled: legs get too warm and cook: Desiree misses another beat: the knuckles pop out of the skin: the fingers open like bananas

Pony: I've proven I look good in a skirt: even the ghosts in my house tell me I look good in a pink skirt: all dance studios are mise-en-abymes, but with long wooden bars across the "abymes": pump-it-up-sing-song: in the mirror, as I'm stretching my left hamstring, my earlobes have become much longer and my nose has become much smaller: almost invisible: where once was a bald chin, I've grown a dry red beard: these are not the results I was promised

Again: outside and semi-still

I believe there is something ridiculously beautiful about men in short-shorts: cotton, mesh, spandex, denim, it all does it right for me: even when the legs aren't shaped right or the butt is flat: an edge of material to the burst of skin: just to glimpse the thigh

A woman on the phone is saying to her friend something I am thinking too: swivel of the hips: the air between us vibrates from this resonance: the embarrassing detail is that what I was thinking and what she said was "what if someone shot up my school tomorrow": swivel of the hips: what happened to women from the 80s: did they ever make it past that last stretch of the video: if only to buy a camcorder and record my friends stretching and chassé-ing, just in case angry boys come with guns: swivel of the hips

I tell myself that I can become Judi Sheppard Missett: however, to do so, I will need an animal sacrifice: right when I slit the throat of the deer, a child throws a rock through my window: it is when my little home is exposed to the small in-pouring of wind that I get distracted and I finish the ritual all wrong: instead of becoming Judi Sheppard Missett, I am just a boy in a leotard and I have an awful deer corpse to clean

Jazzercise is flatland: Jazzercise is new materialism: Jazzercise is your sister: I was pushed into the arms of white women like an angry seagull is pushed away from beach sandwiches: just a wagging of the hand: the sour smell of another person's locker: the same smell for which the Trojan War was fought

Vertical flow of the squat: rhythm as a grabbing hand: I am trying to make my body less present, and for that lesson I pivot my foot: the pivot of an argument: I am much less latino when I am with latinos and I am much less white when I am with white people: I am much less a man when I am around men and I am much less a woman when I am around women: a musical comes with vibrato, by definition: I punch my teeth out while I watch the second VHS in the series: part three, medium cardiovascular to waistline: I hit reset, I hit reset, I'd like to watch, I'd love to watch

What I thought was golden leather fern, strangler fig, sawgrass, melaleuca, milkweed, fogfruit, jasmine, palm, croton, sage, or mango is actually a woman, the one on the left in the chartreuse leotard with white warmers, named Flora.

Caramel swing: show me how music works: I stretch my quadricep into the next room: Judi, Chloe, Desiree, Britney, Linda, Diane, Richard, Annie: everybody dances and everybody is watching: I want to live in the house that Jazzercise built: I own fourteen fancy cars: I have competence in creating my own borders: I flatten my feet: I label everything in my house that is not me as "homegrown"

When the body is small and square: perfect white squares along the highway: singing in rounds new Latin: one neon yellow headband blurs into another: one tank-top strap gets caught in another: the leotard gives a nasty wedgie, floss in teeth

Again:

I determine the circumstance of my own abduction: muscles replicate: what is it like to be Judi Sheppard Missett: to be stoic, strong, kitsch, and clean, to move the body from one place to another, like I move my brain from one sack to another: to stretch the calf from one world to another: when young, the blonde hair mirrored the skull, a big curly growth: but now it defines where the skull begins: termites in the house that Jazzercise built

I bring the video into my home like a good date, or someone from the street with the right eyes: that which eats away at my living room from a locked box: "no more people gathering in large groups": steam under the nail: dropping pamphlets, I am watching five women step left then right: exhaustion architecture: a department in a glass bottle: will you melt the seed: send me chills: send me a potable term for viewership

Again: what you forgot

Slip one finger between your thighs: show him to the family: inside a corporation, you find a little cassette: THIRTY MINUTE BODY BURN: it's been a long time since you've had somewhere to play a cassette: search and search and eventually just put the cassette to your ear to listen into it: other than spinning, you hear nothing, feel nothing: bring me to a business: the incorporation of gravity

To the one man in the back lunging, the one with the high-pitched voice: I know your secrets, I've been there too

Being that I am full of hairspray, she asks me several times if I can deliver volume, curls, stiffness: massaging a stack of shells until something hidden inside announces itself: a crab: a deer with teary gray eyes: dimes thrown against the street, only to bounce back up and chant: there is memory loss within the studio: better memory

The world is plain as a bottle of seltzer: being in shape is a great feeling: where "in shape" matches a railroad's track through four-lane city streets: what holds us apart: possum with blue eyes winces on its tip-toes: hissing bubbles: matte finish on a red nail

We're gonna be burning calories for twenty-five minutes: asking once for a curdling white sneaker: two bay laurels a pot: two eyes to mark a day turned into the next: yesterday was a recovery: today is quiet: yesterday was something twenty feet tall: today is the size of a seashell: will you open the can

I ask them to be my sisters: music drips in the abdomen: "below the belt": Jazzercise since its peak in the 1980s has always tried to stay current, usually translating to current blackness, current Latin-ness: in the late 80s and early 90s Jazzercise sheds its coat of smooth sax-driven jazz and bop and resets to industrial funk, hip-hop: since 2010 Jazzercise has incorporated contemporary pop hip-hop and Latin dance music popular in competitor Zumba: a recent advertising tagline from Jazzercise states "you think you know us, but you don't"

Give me a little time: disturbances

I shot a dog, for lack of a better situation: it steamed into the carpet: telling like a lighthouse, her arm raises up in a jumping jack: the bracelet catches a cube of air: "imagining hazards more awful than real": wife of the anaerobe: I am not changed, I am married

Thick yellow cream across the eyes: quick squats: pulled edge of the mouth: red of Michelle: chest press: one long shot speaking through a water cooler: at just the right angle, you can catch the glimmer of a blue skyscraper just over Jane Fonda's head: past the Venetian windows: blue of Diane: move out: true beige: the pigeon there, at the left corner

If you smile, it makes the workout easier: very slowly, a development of plot: a bone-dry flute's note rolls over the shoulder: only to give it away: snares tighten the abs: for the first part of the exercise, you don't need to use your chair: latch on to me, latch on to me

You did a great job: I am doing the wrong routine in the wrong studio: am I in my hometown: no, shoulder rolls leave room for a gasp between roads: singles and doubles and reach and pull: I am lunging my left leg into Canada, so that Justin Trudeau can kiss my toes: Jane Fonda marches out, her neighborhood was enraged: long bodies: the point of gentle tension

Walk right to me: two sisters of mine stand to my right and left: we were born in a fishbowl: we grew up eating Cheerios: we loved our husbands: but unlike them, I cheated on my husband: they found out: they told him and he left me: they forced me to move to another city: I took on a new name, I took on a new face: I don't blame them for what they did, any good citizen of our hometown would have done the same: I really don't hold a grudge

A tense cold comes through our air conditioner: you pull off my shirt in haste: outlines: even in the dark like this, I can see where your hair starts: your throat expands to hold something warm: stretch my back until it cracks: I cage your thigh with my wet fingers, blue and gold nails: after I suggest we switch, you agree: the yawning of a poster soon to fall from the wall distracts me, but only for a moment

If I was one to tell a lie, which I am not, I would tell it about the fit of a belt around my waist, saying it cinches tighter than it really does, because in my mind, the secret of a circular thing is necessary to keep away from those who ask: moving-with, velocity of a spiral: almost graceful

Fingers on a silk screen: chin depression: touch of rouge at the corners of the forehead warm the face: a line of white or yellow down the bridge of the nose: what is buried under snow

A room with a leaking battery in the middle: if the ocean was only jellyfish: determine the largeness of a personality: salinization: Maggie, swim it, that's just a plastic bag: for every space I occupy, I bring another space with me from somewhere else

I want my stretches to come naturally: I want to drink my drinks through a silver straw like my father and his father: I want to shave my legs and cover them with fake white hair: I want nipple pasties made of post-it notes that remind me to call the venue after nine: if I were in The Ring, my hair would catch in the space between the bricks of the well

I push my middle finger into one of Richard Simmons's hundred blonde curls: gaps of the fence: tie my whisker to the bed post: a brunette boy with a vision board

Choice of pathways: the knee, like a beetle, protects itself from breeze: in the middle of the studio, dented into the hardwood, is a footprint: Sam sleeps in mustard, imagining a long street, black as what is hidden: slice disco: a major seventh chord sags over Desiree's forehead: single, single, double

Last set: trapezius, deltoids, and triceps: look one way and then another: pieces of the body: harder, more friction: a stretching leg's torrid smell: make me sick: I give away my dirty socks to mollify the spirit I live with: that devil which hath invaded my home

A lizard skates across the room to say "last one":
this is the modified workout for those weak in
the heart: lay my head across your copper arm
hair

Again: pull an ingrown hair from my thigh: proof
I am elated

Can you touch your elbow to your knee: that's awesome: Denise identifies me as the woman to watch: "watch her! watch her if this is too difficult for you": "low-impact" is a reminder that during a workout, any part of our body could snap, tear, and break: however, it also allows access to the injured, disabled, inexperienced, or elderly: where all the others are jumping, I am taking two steps forward and two steps back: this routine really is a puzzler

Top of the arms arc, a single cuff connected to a ceiling lamp: I get dizzy inside a cartwheel, my ears start ringing: a warm, high squawk from the air conditioner: my spine becomes misaligned: my lover tells me my eyes are getting completely white: I say it is an illusion of sugar

Here is the decathlon: orange light flickers off the sweat on your brow: give the legs rest, she says: squeeze, tighten, square: I push my fist into the neck of the bottle: here, against the gold-coated office building, I lift my ass into the air

Keep me parallel: bad thoughts

Judi Sheppard Missett says "you don't want to be lopsided" with a crescent smile: the Bar-Kays soar over Judi's waistline routine: her quotes from the song a distant stimulation: you gotta boogie with this honey: stretch-out: move your boogie body: threatened in a day-lit street

You really fear Diana Krall: you always have my unspoken passion: shaking legato of the alto sax shifts loose hair: slur: Nina has the chin of a rabbit, the voice of an angel, and short words: bottled water

Telecommunications: the shrinking spine: what is smaller becomes more concerted: am I a figment of my own vision: a paper plane: promoted

Shannon's arms are overdetermined: olive oil clinging to the plastic bowl: bright screen: I lick the fish until it bends

Holes: no child lagging: blue ammunition: lower home: at best, I am a worldling as unintelligible as curtains: something brown floating at the top of the infinity pool

Must I always be a stranger to you: arrangement of blocks: mind me: turning blue beneath the eyes

A dog with mange has been chewing at the right leg of the coffee table: its ears have an orange tinge: I pull up a chair to offer it meat: 2D skyline, hanging from a cherry sky: a rouge triangle, just under the ear

Do this with me: place a piece of blue painter's tape across the entirety of your thigh: then, rip it off: repeat until you don't pull anymore hairs from that spot: then, move to the next spot on your thigh: if it becomes too sore, rub a bit of cold rosemary water over the affected area: for lower impact, replace blue painter's tape with several sticky notes

The vein, the misshapen god: my fingers wag when I am not looking: her right shoulder flickers in and out of my home: a white hand sifts through a pile of red beans and squash

She rejects a mindless purpose: calls a calf down: in order to be mindful of common sorrow: potion: the fingers develop the draft, coming from the wet, exposed corner of the studio: cold portion

"Give the stars to me": doling out senses of friction: control panel: touched by me: moves: in the airport, I hope not to see anyone I know: I want to get to my gate and sit and read and not have to talk to anyone: I want to go home that way

The ankle sprains: the ACL tears: the quads strain: the hamstrings pull: the abdominal muscles tear: the obliques tear: the soleus ruptures: something unsure snaps: the shoulder dislocates: you get a concussion: you go to sleep: pale ends of petals: the head heals: the shoulder pops back into place: something unsure mends: the soleus heals: the obliques heal: the abdominals heal: the hamstrings are relieved: the quads are relieved: the ACL heals: the ankle heals

Again: the sound of hair being pulled: inversion from the root

You, at home, move with me: move almost before me: I am shaking involuntarily, the way you have always known me to do when I am angry or sad or horny or bitter or embarrassed: you grip me until I stop: like Proteus: a lycra band wiggles and travels from the neck to the crotch

A friend of mine once left a video paused on his TV so long the still image burned into the plasma: anything he ever watched from then on had the faint whisper of that long shot over it: I finger the TV screen, plasma parting around me as I swipe: velvet lake: potential state of reappearance: wash your hair over me

Here, in my room, a chirping sound from the shell of the alarm: I am stretching my leg onto the wooden bar, where the woman next to me spreads like a radiator: she cracks her fingers on my back: low resolution: I bite the skin out from under my nail

I want another moment with my family before trial: I want softer skin below my eyes: I want thin legs that snap when I run: I want a blue light shining across my sideburns: the pink of her headband spreads onto her skin: gemstone: white outline

The breath: the anaerobe in hallucinogenic oxygen: swollen joints quickly deflate: pierced balloon and basket: six white women stepping to the left: the mouth shapes along the deepest curve in the breath: composition: I occupy someone else's seat again: a whistle that sinks from B♭ to G# only to return a moment later

Again: queen of spades: missive: tower of glass

Again: I miss an old friend: another killing: the sickness that sinks below the teeth: I hold onto my problems like a heap of fish: slipping out onto my shoes: I want a remote that changes the direction of my toes: an adjustable brace to change the circumference at the wide end of my head: a lever to pull my spine tighter: loss, as Judi says, is the state of having something from your hands become wild: we meet between counts: center of the afternoon

Again: the sound of a body being thrown to the ground: four on the floor

I want to wish out
a lacy cream
a hope of
non-regulation
the easy way to
slip through the fingers
a vision of
wheat white across
the field an owned field
not to run across
for danger of shots
I am being told there is
a ghost under my bed
I am being told the
fridge is full of bugs I
ittle drops
on the exercise mat
I did not wipe
down my station
the mark that
I was there

Take five marbles
place them in a glass
fill the glass with mud
do something else
for enough time
that the marbles
begin to sprout
hair in the sun
comb them
spray them
so they stiffen
this will tone the thighs
tighten the waist

I do not relate
to boys in other cities
or if the paper sliced
a kite a made thing
limp as cotton
part of what pours into
the wound
a bullet
let it go through
a city's name
the rat
bites at cords
lycra wilderness the
future is full of them
not just a genie but
deviant rhythms
my brow lowers
straightens
my hand reaches
the strings
in my wrist
tangle and harden
the open stones at the
edge of the hand
but a song lies
sweetly on the
wound

Fill a bathtub
with hot water
place the doilies
from your dinner set in it
three drops of red dye
and seven drops of
jasmine oil
put your hand
in the water
let it soak until dawn
peel off the
skin of your hand
until you see
white underneath
this will strengthen
the joints
and improve our grip

It gradually melts
one and the other
flour and chocolate
leotard left in a safe
the gullet shaping
up the account
of a crime the
activity between men
that which is
secret and held
between the eyes
he hits below the belt

Let all your friends
know the same secret
about your personality
then change
that aspect of yourself
without telling them
in this way
the secret is still yours
but they will see you
more clearly
this will strengthen
your squat
and open your breath

I was wrong
whipped oil
into rings
exhausted from work
and lifting
into studio lights
the yolk in the eye
horror of an area
assembling sharp
parts wax thigh
the fixture above
that dissolves
and dissolves

Boil water in a lead pot
let the metal
soak into the water
pour it into a glass
and serve it
to your husband
do this again
then wait
ask him
how he is feeling
do this once a day
this will help us
to reduce
our problem areas

Clicks atop
the foot
measure howled
lumps that form
on my cheeks when
my skin is wet
Judi's nails taped to
the white board
bowl of white grease
win me a prize
every time
you sleep around
and sweat
give me my thirty
minutes
with my feet against
the window

In front of the mirror
change the size
of your fingers
make them very short
or very long
thick or thin
lumpy or smooth
observe your friends
and lovers react
to your new fingers
observe them very closely
do this several times
over the course of a week
this will improve blood flow
and regulate the pulse

Mine is gold
won't you show me
yours howling
into paper
a yellow slug
I have for a tongue
I have asked
God to make my
legs look more like
Puerto Rico
I have hairy
orange stiff things
under these warmers
doing it all
together

Google a photograph of
your favorite author
and print many copies out
place them in between
the pages of every
book you own
under your pillow
below dinner mats
in the lining of jackets
continue this way
for fourteen days
after this time
you will begin to feel
lighter and softer
and eventually still quieter
skinnier faster
this will keep you alert
and help us trim
excess belly fat

The brain is an
inconsolable
portrait hoping
for protection
from an empty room
shaved ice
with red ink she's got
a tattoo with all
the pepsi colors
for wanting more
for wanting
more support
knuckles against
aluminum foil
scabs scraping off
moving her waist
like a top spinning
over marble
motes in light

As you begin to fall
asleep imagine
a star low-
hanging right
above your nose
just as intense
but small enough
to fit in your room
glue things
to your star
like paper scissors clay
cups hair bedsheets
plastic toys
until your star is totally
covered
and your room
is dark again
this will help us
tighten those
pesky love
handles

Events have the
misfortune of perishing
stubborn
as horizontal pressure
these intervals
between my
exhaustion
and the perfect
instructor's smile
are a trace
of force I am constantly
lagging
behind the instructor
tangling my legs
moving my hips in the
wrong direction
I want triangular grace
and the tangent on
the curve

Mix flour and water
to create a tough dough
pull it into
the shapes
of close friends
send each of your friends
the version of
themselves you have
restlessly molded
ask them to send back
the bread if the likeness
is not immediate
and try again
this will help you
keep up with our
more advanced steps

Heart of palm
softly sliced into
I am told to search
for "practice"
among tissues
a long brown bed
a long white person

Write down
your lover's thoughts
at night while
he is sleeping
surprise him by writing
them on his
bedroom walls
when he wakes up
he will be reminded
of times he has felt
without control
and will be consoled
continue this process
and publish his thoughts
in four volumes when he
has finally passed away
this will keep you feeling
healthy happy
and full of energy

I am at several points
not gripped to
God or silk
a liver tied against
a cork-board frame
like an animal trophy
on a mantle
this simple article
or a saxophone
alive again
that I have not asked
for or wanted in this
part of the house
I am not expensive
as city rooms

Pour lotion or
cocoa butter
into a bathtub
sleep inside
and once
you wake up
and they are soft enough
cut off your skin tags
with nail clippers
this will help us
speed your
incredible growth

The way that home
goes invisible
under pressure
the same way then
the taffy
loosens up
to the six the nine
million more
mobile
tongues and flies
round glass cylinder
turning darker
and thinner
an implication of
summer

During the next rain
let five rye
loaves dissolve on
the lawn
collect the leftover
masses and grow them
in a glass
until they form
a golden-brown tower
this will help us
imagine what you
would look like
in a test tube

She cuts the
soft white
underside
of my foot
and it all
just spills out
from the ache
the slit
I deflate very
quickly
and become
inexcusable
so be it
for the apartment
is as ugly
as I dreamed
and more

Count the steps
from your bed
to your shower
to your kitchen
to your backyard
then try to cut out
as many steps
as possible
bring things closer
stretch your
legs farther
remove
extraneous walls
this will keep you
feeling tall and
in charge

A collapsing
building is
never alien to
me nor are the
prices of
damages there was
an accident and
it was clean
and something paused
and something else
resumed

If it is a windy
month thank the
nearest flight
attendant
for their service
ask them if it is easy
to tell passengers
how to put on
breathing masks
and then thank
the nearest breathing
mask
this is a great
exercise for carpal
tunnel pain

I am saddest in
the winter
everything inflates
with cold air
in Judi Sheppard
Missett's house
the infinity
pool freezes over
the white
platter of the
yard her chandelier
becomes very brittle
and sometimes drops
shards onto the dining
table ironically the
freezer is the only
section of the home
she feels she can trust
that and the
underarm
of her daughter
still sixteen even on
the warmest day
of winter

Send everyone
away send your
cousins away
sell your
things sell your
home kill your
pets free-up your
schedule ruin your
relationship and break
a hundred porcelain plates
get rid of everything
including that
troublesome belly fat

The matter over
a long slapped
bass note
cylinders stains
Venetian blinds or
popsicle sticks
smell of the studio
metallic lemongrass
who is keeping
Richard Simmons in
his home and why
won't he talk to
all his beautiful friends
they want to know
is it Teresa

Leave on
the rice
cooker
Leave on
the rice
cooker

Whatever feels good
if you pivot your
feet here and
here and smiling now
if you want to you
can hold it
there and then turn it
back out
and don't bend it
more than you feel is
right here it is
the marathon and
if you've got a
weaker back
you can feel
the spinning of
the spine
and the smooth
air the brass
bell broccoli
and the love of
salt

Just watch
me and do what
I do I'll let you
know what you
need to do
and frequently
discuss the "lighter side"
so you can see
how to make this easier
if at any point you
begin to feel a burning
sensation in your muscles
keep going this is a
signal that your body
refuses change

She played "Sweet
Georgia Brown" for
coordination
and ate Raisinets
off-camera
I shifted my weight
and then tapped my
foot shift tap shift tap
shift tap with a little
extra bounce I squared
my hips to the floor
and put my elbows
into a hot bowl
I always
wear supportive
footwear so I can
turn any way I please

Listen to her breath
between words quick
and shifty a record scratch
replicate her breath
tighten your abs
do this in
your bed while looking up
at the popcorn ceiling
where the little silver
lights hang too
and take your hands into
your throat
this will help
the beginners
among us

The mambo is a very
sexy step
Cuba is "brimming
with life" says a photo
of thirty men in the
New York Times one
with a cigar
Cuba has a way
of staying hot
we will
land our president
in it the people
there are thick
and round and they
play dominos and they
are black sometimes
and white other times
and royal blue is their
favorite color the
mambo is a
very sexy step

One more: last night
I saw you dreaming you'd
be delicate
and teething
look at me
and trace my nose
on bristol
feel them and make your
body a full circle
the island does
not come with a stamp
of joy
this will help us
lengthen the neck
and remember to
drink plenty of water

Open houses my
arms who
has accused
me of being gaudy
I am correcting
for discontentment
invented in my
basement where a
spread of cardboard
is red and orange
and silverfish
make a white S
across the wood
floor the mark that
I was there

Pour
out gallons of milk
on the sidewalk
in honor of
lazy friends
this will help us
square the
shoulders to the
floor

Parking lot long summer the evil eye
you spray blue shiny detergent like a
band of sea-foam red at the end of a
square day full of money of pudding
vapor and highways the gadfly given
their knuckles were made for gloves
I want nobody in my home not a soul
take pictures between strings let the
pale arms beat the linoleum like bell
and marble I hate a lake I eat a stop
sign as if told I could be a receipt it's
felt without corners and velcro with
all the hooks removed I want skinny
fingers a print of rakes slips out of a
knight of cups and vasoline the heat
the fig leaf the chubby kid in a vest
he's like me but I'm an ugly woman

an old man at a carnival who wants

powdered sugar for his kids elephant

ears ice cream fried oreos chocolate

cotton candy sweet jokes for his wife

me the oven he's got an eye the left

on yellow jewels to put in his child's

hair the red the green the black and

if it can be determined I'll make the

case for the hawk the fish a moment

bigger than that left eye I always do

think of you but in moments mobile

homes disguises otherwise swing a

leg over your head get stretched and

ready for a killer workout with me the

only brother you were born with then

the only answer is a street's median

which I will drive over in my red suv I

deserve wet clothing I want the gun the shit stains the blood stains motor boats chopping fat manatees full of a sopping green leaf and there I visit my sister and ask her a favor lend me enough money to make it to the next month just fifteen more days I don't want to think she wouldn't help me but she asks me to scram I terrify I lose fifteen pounds with this regimen and I feel so good I feel like I feel better than ever jello a fish's mouth that's what I want from the 1960s more jello but as I go and get older I hate novelty food items it's an issue of scale y'know take your wrist and push it into my neck roll it around I've got these awful knots my

shoulders are very cold figurehead I

am with my second mind where I die

my head is a cone I am let go free of

devices of imps with curtains let me

make my brain smaller I find myself

most real in a card box god my arm

is always asleep I would cut it off if

just to lose that squirmy ants feeling

it's terrible he has sent me an email

as if that would make me feel better

there I heard an oboe in my sleep

that terrible quack that fuzz and wool

half-hole d gargoyle a penny on the

needle it's boogie it's a two-step as

a monument to finger-licking golden

wings crispy thighs hot oil tight waist

the bottom of the argument keeping

kids around the home like porcelain

swans still life paintings you have

met your family they are in my bottle

light a candle for me light a candle

for my friends canada goose biceps

down feathers triceps lats medium

cardiovascular a week with raquel

she says her stretch is nonviolent

she says I am the armpit of george

bernard shaw what a wish angry

teens dream of sleeping in a car the

warm gray fiber of the armrest want

nervous at the throat what should be

said the judges are looking for four

consecutive push-ups four pull-ups

four high-kicks and four jumping

jacks it is all sponsored by crystal light the competitors are all talented competitors in this competition we're going to have to try our darndest to compete against these competitors I met linda when she was my teacher she had such high energy she grew me like a plant very slowly and with pruning now we can do a split at the same time crystal light my mother cut bangs greg louganis is here he hit his head crystal light is my diet drink of choice dance with me 2 and 2 and 2 mesh 2 and 2 and 2 "women with the upper body strength to do great push-ups" hollywood trolley a coin with a brown band in the middle

two twenty five to ride I lost my egg
and I lost my boyfriend I wave in a
circle I block my eyebrows I cat eye
in black I put soft purple eyeshadow
above I contour my fatty cheek I pull
my teeth I pucker my lips I pull my
hairs my fingers are all thumbs wax
daybreak economic theory sweaty
ass kids fat fucks sweetbreads trade
that split is an amazing achievement
and will net this pair some deserved
points fog parking lot brown coat my
friend has got lice can you believe it
it's like a cartoon I fill myself with
bread I piss between meals my mom
has told me I eat all the bread they
bring I don't rip it and share judi it's a

hot fucking day makes you want to
go pour a glass of wine through your
thighs that's what I would do if I lived
alone ladies and gents your glutes
are like huge banana breads missile
foam thighs the nail smashed and
high standing a guard I don't want to
be a professional dancer I just want
to look like one shanna will eat your
head judi in that cherry-red egg chair
or by that original lichtenstein or the
warhol or your koi pond some idiot
left the family jewels in the koi pond
shanna denise jane richard none of
them can do what you do judi I stuff
my face with a cronut I sleep with
you on my mind my ex had long

fingers and a little belly that he hated
and shook in the mirror I'd smoke
with you if I didn't have bad lungs if I
wasn't very tired if it wasn't 2:47am
as always if it wasn't gooey if I
wasn't playing a game if I cared
about my friends if the q-tip didn't
come out orange if I wasn't about to
puke from too much roast pork I'd
smoke with you hem of the evening
glossy parameter leave me alone in
my room I decorated it for a reason
we'll start from the top now as if we
were rain a late-night icee run at
turkey hill white cherry and coke root
beer barq's to be specific the matter
delivered in address to the general

public twice lived little holes double
vision three of wands my crush we
fall asleep in a film about bowling
rotten places receipts deviance
commissioned by the national
museum of buck teeth work those
hamstrings best joke a friend ever
told me was hamstrings but literally
made of ham like white americas
christmas dinner so easy targets
heal everything we are very soft and
wooden as a leg a hospital has got a
cat that will predict my death silver
sea hand-held vacuum I pinch my
nipples in the mirror to appear taller
raw pinks get orange the hem of my
scapula the seams of my neck judi

sheppard missett is a hundred
squares in a mambo in a grapevine
down the alleyway a guy with pearly
white calloused hands let's start
again one more set piston my history
triple sec long sock the kids are in a
hot car craving fingers anxious about
each other's breaths telling secrets
trading joints keeping watch out the
window those rats my biceps I'm
feeling better than ever I'm feeling
like my best self I keep my best self
in the closet where she is happiest
around plenty plastic hangers and
mothballs I am wearing a girdle
believe me it is aromatic like my
upbringing like my carpentry the

methods of other families my waist
the needs of the dog over mine tube
dress sick shit I'll make it over the
bridge I'll make it into my bowl of
black beans and vaca frita and white
rice and materva as if it was sunday
or good friday and I'll make it into
class to chassé and pivot and I'll
make it into my studio to meet Jane
angry batteries she's tossed her hair
over the bar and develops a warm
rash along the underarm she tells
my friends of my collection she and I
are not hourglasses we are girders
and my toes are soft as cinnamon
jane takes me to the ice cream truck
on 23rd st and there she believes

me she touches my hair I develop a

curse and lose my eyesight I cut into

lesions on my foot which pop like

water balloons I have fallen badly

my kneecap dislocates and juts to

the right a bone in my calf has bent

out of my skin it looks like teeth long

summer stuffed animal deck of cards

I'm burning an effigy to my body at

eighty whether I can still swim like

grannies in articles online or whether

I am frail and broken or already dead

I am burning an effigy to say I am

revolted by what came out of my

dissolving libido correct my spine

length I'm a piñata I'm a stick I want

to be a blonde bombshell I'll crack

open the nose skin tags I am in the

deer carcass sleeping ballroom shed

silversmithing I am out of butter I

can't make eggs I ram the writing

desk into a vacuum watch me as a

carnivore 2 and 2 and 2 and 2 and 2

my copper arm hair your basket if

one discovered the other the plié the

pirouette the cabbage patch the

running man the swim the sprinkler

the worm the bump I have designed

a diorama of myself and my friends

prepared for a turkey dinner clay ear

cauliflowers papier maché eyebrows

eat and turn into a pig like mom and

dad in spirited away but I've got

empanadas and papas rellenas not

ba-wan but lechón and flan and judi

sheppard missett takes an axe to my

wrist leopard print mint julep pattern

blocking his hand-lines his elbow in

my back I pluck out his eyelashes

I'd let him build me a bigger house

marble floors stairs designer lamps

cindy crawford's ghost haunting my

couch a bucket of cold brew on the

frame of the door waiting for my

husband to come home so it can

drop I love his new beard I love his

big arms his yellow head we are iced

tea together violet roads cheetos I've

heard the news you're leaving me

for him even after I've heard you

complain every day about your

friends I was there and I put my pale
thumbs into your neck you slip me
out of my t-shirt glass water-based
pink sweat warm ring chocolate
donut t-bone steak do this with me
stretch your hands out across the
lake and into the house of your
neighbor fluff his pillow drink his milk
rearrange his statuettes so if the
furrowed brow wasn't message for
you enough my lettuce leaf the nap
of the baby marigold mirage you do
know my motored jawline this is the
blue blue of my insecure appraisal
god is so generous about many
things especially my figure I was
taught by marists that he has great

callouses on his god hands and they

will touch me above the forehead

and my body will be very perfect and

muscular kids took their cocks out

in catholic school as if to announce

their divorce from private spaces

another message sent by the pores

step-touch heel back v-step we

might be finding our center here in

the basement between wood slats

the step out a crystal buried in the

soil of a family farm it telegrams my

want my tongue is shaped like a

donut I recycle it again the grain silo

inside my forehead a lazy cloud the

day sends me chills down my ankles

the rumor is inverse gnashing of the

wind-up soldier pink ribbon between

the middle and index fingers what is

a way I percolate in your room I

massage your yolky joke the strip

mall gooey secrets spread on the

cross jesus lovely triceps the ding

dong hostess cakes alive in the

bowling pin the boxcar base I mount

my sullen fingernail and press it with

salty blue ink the sand is nearing

the apartment building I will name it

jacob mispronounced I am the only

scarecrow this family desires take

me as your wife along lincoln road

push me into oncoming traffic I will

laugh in steel a reason more for

letting your grip loosen on her diane

desiree   karen   madeleine   natasha

fiona brittany you have caught the

trumpeter in your catalog make no

mistake my purse is lost upon my

waking the rodeo dynamite the white

crystal legs psuedo-science of car

batteries do this with me and a-one

and a-two and a three-e-and-a-four

I'm made for more I develop black

photos under red light my relief in

clean cardboard the phrasing nested

lightly between pixels sticky sun beat

up ramshackle spartans there is a

great grey hole behind venus that is

sucking gas fast and will leave us

without knees I burp a contrail it

soars across the sky it's true the

light of the sun does meet my skin I
was born to replicate puerto rico I
bankrupt the indigo freeway I have
lost six pounds this week alone I am
committed I am supplementing this
with diet and light weight training
please be sure to supplement this
with diet and light weight training for
the best results I am not transparent
nor am I defensive I am a medical
center I am your best customer I
must be as stuck in your nose as the
q-tip oh jill it's not true I did buy the
oatmeal you asked for I did I spent
my own money on it too no I am not
harassing your secretary I really
believe she is not from this planet

and neither is our son I am only as

glassine as the program allows this

is my two-handed axe my volcanic

suv he thinks he has me to himself

but I am not a bowl of cereal you are

if fairies only knew the horrible smell

of their wings gourmet scallions midi

august I took raw graphite from the

crash of the blimp let your knees

drop to the floor completely smile

and be yourself look straight into the

light chocolate involution always

before always before the sound of

elephants this is my favorite routine

to mark my tibia with red circles then

over some hill there is the rest of the

world my friend would want me to

say this is the truth the sun is
amazing but I am not my friend my
lamp is amazing beta of january the
trial run reverse week mid-waist is
not to be ignored then repeat these
exercises on your own time outside
of class to get closer to your favorite
body you are the mortar and she is
the salad say "approaching" in a
strange accent to relax the mind be
at ease make sure you are breathing
all at the same time leave your arms
right here in my oyster the beach
gifts you reagan garlic knots quarter
frames task men's singlet cradler
white wine with minerals dried fruit
falling from the tree onto her head

the voice is loud there is soil it is not
a myth that cloud there it is bigger
than phalanges and tree nuts that
tree there is skinny I finger the open
notebook drink paper and wine I
puke after a ritual and brush my
teeth this is how I say I am not my
sister nor the metal bowl I'd put a girl
in my direction tape triangle colored
pencils to eat to eat we are lemons
again we are deer we are full of
gucci shoes I feel my heart leap into
tomorrow because I am lonely today
I feel the state of pennsylvania in my
shoulder how many times have I
wished I could talk faster be more
convincing my time here in this video

has been a series of embarrassing
lyrics now that the balls of my feet
ache my head will lower and I will
admit I have no real lover or friend I
am holding onto continents in a
pageant I am wearing the sash of
miss florida my hair in a bump-it I
am beautiful my gown fits me so
perfectly and my answer to how I'd
change the world is precious I even
mention the everglades I am the
crown it is a short day everything is
fast nautical doctrine comments I am
a woman with many hats deliver the
eggs in their brown basket the dog is
alive something is moving slowly
under the asphalt scaly and purple it

is coming to eat out of the toilet of judi sheppard missett's home the embodiment of shanna's anxiety and embarrassment over dinner and poultry the family is lemonade and their nostrils are black moons the parable has told us the raisins are our friends my buns are tight and toned not ash but chalk not a pool cue but my belly button my last secret in this world I wiggle my tush into your slideshow and projector presentation my smile is camera-worthy believe the mollusks when they say my biceps have never been so defined and veiny grace is poured over my forehead like mustard silver

ladle the pink stone I juggle between
toes janelle I am not like you I was
never supposed to be I put you
in my vhs because I believe I can
do syncopation like you with your
tin eyelashes but it's not true I can
hardly get them open crusted over
with golden pollen the tiles are gray
and dusty and linoleum my sacred
cafeteria my lucha mask my eighth
note my husband and I were meant
to be thermometers sea shells but I
have lost my father to gale-force
winds the same that keep your curls
afloat in the studio the guitar is pink
and fuzzy in its high notes I spent
the nighttime with pat methany and

steve reich tonguing at what should
be known of fast movements and
cloudy counterpoint I eat pat's left
ear and his armpit hair not yet even
near full again I eat the fried dough
again I eat the dripping pork again I
eat the smashed plantains again I
eat split peas and sip the frothy soup
what sits in the pearly suitcase what
bathes in the bay of pigs my
mamboing guajiro and his memories
short man deep appetite mate and
music I want to swallow every island
and keep it in my gullet oh god is my
life a sack of beans and hairy arms
blush cortisone clearasil night masks
microbeads sponges rye bread cane

the little neighbor boy and his mom

are disasters paper planes motors

step forward twice turn and squat

keep those legs in the air I want to

see them high in the air yeah you

feel that I know you do feels good

feels right okay let your legs down

and bring your chest up and back

down and up and back down yeah

work that core we want to feel every

muscle in our belly working really

working feel that burn yeah one

more no excuses here folks this is

the last time oh gosh okay stand up

everybody we've had a great class

and a great session I can see those

big beautiful smiles on your faces

yeah woo that was sensational do

you feel good do you feel lighter

stronger I sure do folks catch us next

time for another hour of sweat hard

work and fun dance moves with the

one and only jazzercise cool off with

some light stretches and I'll see you

next time

      let's go jazzercisin'

      exercisin'

      oh let's go jazzercise

      get that tired ol' body off

      of the floor

      let's go jazzercise

      some more

      let's go jazzercise

      jazzercise

I visit my kids in the garage and ask
them to pull me up from the floor I
am heavy and swallowed steel my
son has just invented astroturf I
bend his knees your friends are
missing from their homes they were
plucked out as if by aliens where are
the forty women of that city block I
get caught between dotted notes we
can fly to ypsilanti or austin and start
a new life I was greedy I wanted all
of everything from my straight friends
those angry boys jerking off into
socks their pubes on the toilet seat
they text me at 3am to ask if I'm
up and I answer I am piecing
together the last remains of the flight

crash the pilot blinded by the sun

pink mustard I can feel it here in the

studio I know it is true it's familiar

and it fizzles across the june sky

parking lot long summer the evil eye

JAZZ
ER
CISE
IS A
LAN
G
UAGE

ACKNOWLEDGEMENTS

First thanks to the people who put up Jazzercise tapes on Youtube. Thanks also to the instructors that narrate these classes, most famously Richard Simmons, Jane Fonda, and the incomparable Judi Sheppard Missett.

Thanks to Roberto Harrison, not just for his kind words on the book but for linking me with Lynne. To Lynne DeSilva-Johnson for her endless generosity and for being an amazing partner in talking about crazy ideas. To Liz Barr for the cover image and her kindness. To CA Conrad for his effort to find this book a home and his unwavering support. To Kevin Killian and Sawako Nakayasu for their words on the book. These three blurb writers are all people I deeply respect. To Andy Emitt for early and unwavering confidence in this project.

I wish I could write a thousand pages of thanks to Julia Bloch. This book was written under her guidance: she and I together drafted a reading list (copied on the next page); she gave me helpful notes and edits on the manuscript at various stages of its writing; and she retained an open dialogue with me throughout our months together about various directions the book could and would take. This book would not be near what it is today without her. Thanks to her for tolerating me emailing her about how I wanted form to succeed, not fail, at 3 in the morning and her actually taking it seriously.

Thanks to the editors of the following journals/sites for publishing excerpts from this book: Word Riot, Supplement, Ferrofluid, Hold, Tenderloin, Theme Can 3, and Lambda Literary.

Thanks must always be given to the community at the Kelly Writers House for the intricate conversations made there and for the simple pleasure of being there. As well to the Philadelphia writing community, an amazingly caring web of people who I can't begin to thank individually. Thanks to my family and close friends for their tolerance and love. And as always, nothing less than everything to Jibreel.

POETICS and PROCESS :: a CONVERSATION
with GABRIEL OJEDA-SAGUE
and OS FOUNDER/EDITOR LYNNE DESILVA-JOHNSON

Greetings comrade! Thank you for talking to us about your process today!

Can you introduce yourself, in a way that you would choose?

I'm Gabriel Ojeda-Sague, I'm a Latino, gay poet living in Philly, originally from Miami.

Why are you a poet/writer/artist?

Because I write. I started writing without a clear understanding of why when I was about 16. It was all very bad and I wasn't very committed to it either. Around 19 or so, it clicked more accurately that I was interested in aesthetics and the untrueness of aesthetics. Writing is the field of the arts that I understand the most and have the most love for, so I committed to that craft over the others (though to be fair, I love the others). In doing so, I've found my understanding of poetry as a simulation of language, experience, and aesthetics. The word "simulation" there is key for me because it marks that a poem is not true, and that gap is what I try to exploit the most.

What's a "poet" (or "writer" or "artist") anyway?

Someone who writes what they identify as poetry. I know that's a boring answer, but it is really necessary, because it avoids and contradicts my three least favorite answers to this kind of question: 1) people who refuse to call themselves poets out of embarrassment, insecurity, inexperience, and so they think of poet as a far-away thing 2) people who get overly dramatic and are like "poets are mountains!" or something like that, and 3) people who use poetry as an honorific, like calling songwriters poets just because they have beautiful and complex lyrics. It's insulting to both songwriters and poets. So I want poet to be the person who writes poetry and who interacts with communities of others who are poets. It's as simple as that for me.

What do you see as your cultural and social role (in the literary / artistic / creative community and beyond)?

This is a tough one for me. Ask me this one year ago and I would say that poets don't do anything. That poetry can't enact. This was me being, I think, a bit bitter about the language around "activist" poetics, which I think is often insulting. Nowadays, I'm really not sure. So my answer is, I don't know. In the artistic community, it is just about continuing, evolving, transforming, and making conversations around the aesthetic, social, environmental, political, emotional, ontological, epistemological, and/or the semiotic. To the rest of the world? I can't figure it out. Maybe it just has to do with making someone think differently for the time they are interacting with your work.

Talk about the process or instinct to move these poems (or your work in general) as independent entities into a body of work. How and why did this happen? Have you had this intention for a while? What encouraged and/or confounded this (or a book, in general) coming together? Was it a struggle?

I really think I'm at my best in a book. When I write page poems, I make them strong and inconclusive because I am very against the idea of the whole poem, the poem that ends with applause, the tight drawstring bag poem. As well, it has to do with the business of poetry too, since the big lit mags thrive off of writing that can live inside one page. I've been moving towards long poems and book projects for some years now because I think there is something much more humane about the process of book-making, especially alongside a smart and kind press that knows what it is doing. Instead of, hey I write this and I send it to the Kenyon Review or some shit and I pay whatever the read fee is and then it gets rejected and 10,000 people are also doing this and none of us win out because they are going to solicit 15 out of the 20 people that will be in their new issue anyways. So the book or the body of work has never scared me, in fact it's freed my thinking and made it more concrete.

Did you envision this collection as a collection or understand your process as writing or making specifically around a theme while the poems themselves were being written / the work was being made? How or how not?

This book started with the title of it. I showed my friend a funny mash-up video of Judi Sheppard Missett quotes and me and her were talking about the way she speaks and how specific her words are. And at some point I kinda just said "yeah, Jazzercise is like its own language" and thought "hey wait a minute!" And so I had a title and I knew I wanted to write a poetry book about Jazzercise and its language and I thought okay well what's the argument of the book. And so over some thinking, I started writing a few pages of it. I looked at what was happening in the pages that I wrote and thought, okay I think I understand my argument. I think I know what I'm thinking in this poem. Then, I asked the poet Julia Bloch to organize with me and help me format my thinking. We did it as an "independent study" and I wrote and she helped me understand where the project was going and we shared a lot of dialogue about it. And bam.

What formal structures or other constrictive practices (if any) do you use in the creation of your work? Have certain teachers or instructive environments, or readings/writings/ work of other creative people informed the way you work/write?

Reference the above for the literal structure of writing this. Julia and I came up with a "syllabus" (a tool I have been continuing to use in new projects) of readings that might guide me while I was writing. Lots of amazing books that I read and reference and wrote towards and away from. The only constrictive practices were the forms in the poem. The poem has 3 forms. The first is a "paragraph" of justified prose, with phrases divided by colons. The second is two crescents of writing, one left aligned, one right aligned, with the right aligned part positioned three lines lower than the left. The third is a justified column of continuous text with 3 lines of space between each line of text.

All of these had exact margin measurements that I worked out, but I can't remember the numbers right now. But it was very exacting. So the text had to fit inside of these structures in appealing ways, causing some words to not be usable in certain places. For example, in the third section say I wanted a line that said "bla bla bla I am on the freeway" but the word freeway was too long, causing it to go over the justification margin meaning the entire word freeway would move to the next line and the words "bla bla bla I am on the" would be stretched out by the justification algorithm. That wouldn't work for me, visually, so I picked a different word. So these algorithms change the text. It's a bit like slicing off limbs, but that has an appeal in and of itself. Aesthetically, not medically.

Speaking of monikers, how does your process of naming (individual pieces, sections, etc) influence you and/or color your work specifically, beyond this text?

I will say that a title is really important to me. A good title can really help a book and a bad title can really ruin it. For example, I really hate those titles that are in vogue with lots of poets that are like "How to put a bottle back together, or you called me last night but I was busy watching Real Housewives so I ignored it." I mean, I can't stand them. For a while, I thought "Jazzercise is a Language" might be too overdramatic, but then I thought HELLO we're talking about Jazzercise! It's all meant to be tacky so I'm keeping it.

I think my favorite title of mine was for a short story I wrote a while back (I have a negative relationship to the 4 short stories I wrote, published two. I don't really write short stories anymore but, who knows, maybe I'll return to it), which was called "Milk for Lulu with Child," which was about a gay teen boy giving milk to a teen girl who was pregnant. It's literally just a description of the plot, but it does its job. Also, I currently like the title of a poem that I wrote recently called "Lanes," it's about that game Plants v Zombies which is a lane-defense game, but it is also a pun on "Lines" which is the title of oh so many poems. I like titles like that. Simple, descriptive, turn the work only slightly and don't stab at it.

What does this particular work represent to you. as indicative of your method/creative practice?

I think it is the best example of my practice of writing on viewer-experience of different forms of media. This has been my main theme for sometime and motivates my chapbooks on The Joy of Gay Sex, Cher's twitter, and The Legend of Zelda, as well as some individual poems like my poem on The Binding of Isaac. I think "Jazzercise is a Language" is the most accomplished my thinking on these subjects has been thus far.

What does this book DO (as much as what it says or contains)?

This book is a way of interpreting and closely investigating the way the aesthetics of Jazzercise, camp, neon, aerobics, intersect with Jazzercise's racial/body politics through the lens of a Latino, gay, gender-discordant viewer subject (hey, that's me!).

What would be the best possible outcome for this book? What might it do in the world, and how will its presence as an object facilitate your creative role in your community and beyond? What are your hopes for this book, and for your practice?

I want people to read it and I want people to see that the media we shrug off as not-worthy of interpretation can and should be taken seriously and critically. This is not to say there's no fun in it, and actually I think there's a lot of fun in the book! But let's not pretend that we should let anything stand as it is.

I'd be curious to hear some thoughts on the challenges we face in speaking and publishing across lines of race, age, privilege, social/cultural background, and sexuality within the community, vs. the dangers of remaining and producing in isolated "silos."

This is a huge question, with so many different answers and so many topics to cover, many of which I have experienced myself as a Latino person, as a gay person, as a gender-discordant person, as the child of exiles from Cuba, etc. My philosophy in short has been that we need to work against the network, the web of dominant connections that the literary world rides on, continues to manifest, and uses at the expense of other producing nodes. I think its near impossible for your average young person, no formal training, low publication count, to get a book published in a respected press. The problem here is manifold, the problem here is the idea that one must rely on the respected press, the problem here is that people mine the

MFAs lists for people to solicit, the problem here is that editors invite the same people other editors are publishing because they know they are good already, the problem here is that the young person can only get that book published with down and dirty networking skills that a lot of people don't have, the problem here is that you have to put in 50 times the work and effort to get to the career point that somebody else is at where they can put in minimal effort and still get a really nice publishing deal, the problem here is that big presses solicit the same authors again and again and again, the problem here is that everybody is so hungry for that success that so many people forget that they have a local community of writers who are doing great work and that the only thing you need to do to collaborate with those people is show up to a quiet bar reading and open your ears, the problem here is manifold.

Is there anything else we should have asked, or that you want to share?

I want to mention that the performance of this book includes me in full Jazzerciser drag, lip-synching to Judi Sheppard Missett videos. Fun for the whole family, as they say.

JAZZERCISE READING LIST

Below is the reading list Julia Bloch and I drafted that guided me as I wrote. We divided the list into sections that focus on different purposes for the work's inclusion. I have added a few works that were not part of our official reading list, but that also were in my mind during the process. I place it here for your viewing because I believe this transparency is useful towards the reading of the book. And perhaps you might find something you like.

WATCHING EXERCISE VIDEOS

"Fitness is a Feminist Issue" - Tara Brabazon
Shifting Time and Space: The Story of Videotape - Eugene Marlow, Eugene Secunda
Killer Tapes and Shattered Screens: Video Spectatorship from VHS to File-Sharing - Caetlin Benson-Allot
"Where is the Jazz in Jazzercise?" - Sherrie Tucker
"Down with Disembodiment; or, Musicology and the Material Turn" - Holly Watkins, Melina Esse
The Feminism and Visual Culture Reader
Mature Themes - Andrew Durbin
"Queer Exercises" - David Getsy
"Becoming an Image," "Cuts: A Traditional Sculpture" - (Heather) Cassils
Relationscapes - Erin Manning
Grapefruit - Yoko Ono
Ecodeviance - CAConrad

RACE, OR SEEING YOURSELF IN OTHERS

White Girls - Hilton Als
Ban en Banlieue - Bhanu Kapil
S*PeRM**K*T - Harryette Mullen
Dream Machine - Sade Murphy
Empathy - Mei-mei Berssenbrugge
Disidentifications: Queers of Color and the Performance of Politics - Jose Muñoz
Remember to Wave - Kaia Sand
Action Kylie - Kevin Killian
Letters to Kelly Clarkson - Julia Bloch

FORM

Titanic - Cecilia Corrigan
The Battlefield Where the Moon Says I Love You - Frank Stanford
Estilo - Dolores Dorantes
Midwinter Day - Bernadette Mayer

GABRIEL OJEDA-SAGUE is a Miami <-> Philly gay, Latino Leo living in Philadelphia, PA. He is the author of the poetry books *Jazzercise is a Language* (The Operating System, 2018) and *Oil and Candle* (Timeless, Infinite Light, 2016). He is also the author of chapbooks on gay sex, Cher, the Legend of Zelda, and anxious bilingualism. His third book *Losing Miami*, on the potential sinking of Miami due to climate change and sea level rise, is forthcoming from Civil Coping Mechanisms.

The Operating System uses the language "print document" to differentiate from the book-object as part of our mission to distinguish the act of documentation-in-book-FORM from the act of publishing as a backwards-facing replication of the book's agentive *role* as it may have appeared the last several centuries of its history. Ultimately, I approach the book as TECHNOLOGY: one of a variety of printed documents (in this case, bound) that humans have invented and in turn used to archive and disseminate ideas, beliefs, stories, and other evidence of production.

Ownership and use of printing presses and access to (or restriction of printed materials) has long been a site of struggle, related in many ways to revolutionary activity and the fight for civil rights and free speech all over the world. While (in many countries) the contemporary quotidian landscape has indeed drastically shifted in its access to platforms for sharing information and in the widespread ability to "publish" digitally, even with extremely limited resources, the importance of publication on physical media has not diminished. In fact, this may be the most critical time in recent history for activist groups, artists, and others to insist upon learning, establishing, and encouraging personal and community documentation practices. Hear me out.

With The OS's print endeavors I wanted to open up a conversation about this: the ultimately radical, transgressive act of creating PRINT /DOCUMENTATION in the digital age. It's a question of the archive, and of history: who gets to tell the story, and what evidence of our life, our behaviors, our experiences are we leaving behind? We can know little to nothing about the future into which we're leaving an unprecedentedly digital document trail — but we can be assured that publications, government agencies, museums, schools, and other institutional powers that be will continue to leave BOTH a digital and print version of their production for the official record. Will we?

As a (rogue) anthropologist and long time academic, I can easily pull up many accounts about how lives, behaviors, experiences — how THE STORY of a time or place — was pieced together using the deep study of correspondence, notebooks, and other physical documents which are no longer the norm in many lives and practices. As we move our creative behaviors towards digital note taking, and even audio and video, what can we predict about future technology that is in any way assuring that our stories will be accurately told – or told at all? How will we leave these things for the record?

In these documents we say:
  WE WERE HERE, WE EXISTED, WE HAVE A DIFFERENT STORY

- Lynne DeSilva-Johnson, Founder/Managing Editor,
THE OPERATING SYSTEM, Brooklyn NY 2017

TITLES IN THE PRINT: DOCUMENT COLLECTION

An Absence So Great and Spontaneous It Is Evidence of Light - Anne Gorrick [2018]
The Book of Everyday Instruction - Chloe Bass [2018]
Executive Orders Vol. II - a collaboration with the Organism for Poetic Research [2018]
One More Revolution - Andrea Mazzariello [2018]
The Suitcase Tree - Filip Marinovich [2018]
Chlorosis - Michael Flatt and Derrick Mund [2018]
Sussuros a Mi Padre - Erick Sáenz [2018]
Sharing Plastic - Blake Nemec [2018]
The Book of Sounds - Mehdi Navid (Farsi dual language, trans. Tina Rahimi) [2018]
In Corpore Sano : Creative Practice and the Challenged Body [Anthology, 2018];
Lynne DeSilva-Johnson and Jay Besemer, co-editors
Abandoners - Lesley Ann Wheeler [2018]
Jazzercise is a Language - Gabriel Ojeda-Sague [2018]
Return Trip / Viaje Al Regreso; Dual Language Edition -
Israel Dominguez,(trans. Margaret Randall) [2018]
Born Again - Ivy Johnson [2018]
Attendance - Rocío Carlos and Rachel McLeod Kaminer [2018
Singing for Nothing - Wally Swist [2018]
The Ways of the Monster - Jay Besemer [2018]
Walking Away From Explosions in Slow Motion - Gregory Crosby [2018]
Field Guide to Autobiography - Melissa Eleftherion [2018]
CHAPBOOK SERIES 2018 : Greater Grave - Jacq Greyja; Needles of Itching Feathers -
Jared Schlickling; Want-Catcher - Adra Raine; We, The Monstrous - Mark DuCharme

Lost City Hydrothermal Field - Peter Milne Greiner [2017]
An Exercise in Necromancy - Patrick Roche [Bowery Poetry Imprint, 2017]
Love, Robot - Margaret Rhee[2017]
La Comandante Maya - Rita Valdivia (dual language, trans. Margaret Randall) [2017]
The Furies - William Considine [2017]
Nothing Is Wasted - Shabnam Piryaei [2017]
Mary of the Seas - Joanna C. Valente [2017]
Secret-Telling Bones - Jessica Tyner Mehta [2017]
CHAPBOOK SERIES 2017 : INCANTATIONS
featuring original cover art by Barbara Byers
sp. - Susan Charkes; Radio Poems - Jeffrey Cyphers Wright; Fixing a Witch/Hexing the
Stitch - Jacklyn Janeksela; cosmos a personal voyage by carl sagan ann druyan steven
sotor and me - Connie Mae Oliver
Flower World Variations, Expanded Edition/Reissue - Jerome
Rothenberg and Harold Cohen [2017]
What the Werewolf Told Them / Lo Que Les Dijo El Licantropo -
Chely Lima (trans. Margaret Randall) [2017]
The Color She Gave Gravity - Stephanie Heit [2017]
The Science of Things Familiar - Johnny Damm [Graphic Hybrid, 2017]

agon - Judith Goldman [2017]
To Have Been There Then / Estar Alli Entonces - Gregory Randall
(trans. Margaret Randall) [2017]

Instructions Within - Ashraf Fayadh [2016]
Arabic-English dual language edition; Mona Kareem, translator
Let it Die Hungry - Caits Meissner [2016]
A GUN SHOW - Adam Sliwinski and Lynne DeSilva-Johnson;
So Percussion in Performance with Ain Gordon and Emily Johnson [2016]
Everybody's Automat [2016] - Mark Gurarie
How to Survive the Coming Collapse of Civilization [2016] - Sparrow
CHAPBOOK SERIES 2016: OF SOUND MIND
*featuring the quilt drawings of Daphne Taylor
Improper Maps - Alex Crowley; While Listening - Alaina Ferris;
Chords - Peter Longofono; Any Seam or Needlework - Stanford Cheung

TEN FOUR - Poems, Translations, Variations [2015]- Jerome Rothenberg, Ariel
Resnikoff, Mikhl Likht
MARILYN [2015] - Amanda Ngoho Reavey
CHAPBOOK SERIES 2015: OF SYSTEMS OF
*featuring original cover art by Emma Steinkraus
Cyclorama - Davy Knittle; The Sensitive Boy Slumber Party Manifesto
- Joseph Cuillier; Neptune Court - Anton Yakovlev; Schema - Anurak Saelow
SAY/MIRROR [2015; 2nd edition 2016] - JP HOWARD
Moons Of Jupiter/Tales From The Schminke Tub [plays, 2014] - Steve Danziger

CHAPBOOK SERIES 2014: BY HAND
Pull, A Ballad - Maryam Parhizkar; Can You See that Sound - Jeff Musillo
Executive Producer Chris Carter - Peter Milne Greiner;
Spooky Action at a Distance - Gregory Crosby;

CHAPBOOK SERIES 2013: WOODBLOCK
*featuring original prints from Kevin William Reed
Strange Coherence - Bill Considine; The Sword of Things - Tony Hoffman;
Talk About Man Proof - Lancelot Runge / John Kropa; An Admission as a Warning
Against the Value of Our Conclusions -Alexis Quinlan

DOC U MENT
/däkyəmənt/

First meant "instruction" or "evidence," whether written or not.

noun - a piece of written, printed, or electronic matter that provides information or evidence or that serves as an official record
verb - record (something) in written, photographic, or other form
synonyms - paper - deed - record - writing - act - instrument

[*Middle English, precept, from Old French, from Latin documentum, example, proof, from docre, to teach; see dek- in Indo-European roots.*]

Who is responsible for the manufacture of value?

Based on what supercilious ontology have we landed in a space where we vie against other
creative people in vain pursuit of the fleeting credibilities of the scarcity economy,
rather than freely collaborating and sharing openly with each other
in ecstatic celebration of MAKING?

While we understand and acknowledge the economic pressures and fear-mongering
that threatens to dominate and crush the creative impulse,
we also believe that ***now more than ever***
we have the tools to relinquish agency via cooperative means,
fueled by the fires of the Open Source Movement.

**Looking out across the invisible vistas of that rhizomatic parallel country
we can begin to see our community beyond constraints,
in the place where intention meets
resilient, proactive, collaborative organization.**

Here is a document born of that belief, sown purely of imagination and will.
When we document we assert.
We print to make real, to reify our being there.
When we do so with mindful intention to address our process,
to open our work to others, to create beauty in words in space,
to respect and acknowledge the strength of the page we now hold physical,
a thing in our hand… we remind ourselves that, like Dorothy:
we had the power all along, my dears.

THE PRINT! DOCUMENT SERIES
is a project of
the trouble with bartleby
in collaboration with
the operating system